The Complete

Air Fryer Cookbook for Beginners

Learn to Be an Air Fryer Expert with Straightforward and Tasty Recipes You Can Make at Home

Wilona Woods

TABLE OF CONTENTS

PIZZA, BREAD, WRAPS AND SANDWICHES   96

INTRODUCTION

The fryer's unusual nature allows it to heat to incredibly high temperatures, allowing it to fry, roast, and boil food with just a tablespoon of oil. The air-deep frying pan will give the food a delicious, crispy, fried texture that cooks just as well from the inside as a deep fryer by combining only the little bit of oil. Since the passage of hot air allows an air cooker to cook at a much lower temperature than deep-frying, you just need a little oil for your fried food to get the delicious crispy taste of the fry from foo foo. Furthermore, roasting in the air does not produce as much of a fried food odor as frying does.

Of course, a batch of fries is one of the first things you'll want to do with a deep fryer. If you're buying it to use as a key to more veggies, test a few different recipes to see if you like the result. It will also lead to a more nutritious diet because it eliminates the need to abruptly adjust the flavor and consistency of vegetables to that of air-fried vegetables.

You can save a lot of calories by using deep fryers instead of traditional frying. Deep fryers require considerably less oil than conventional frying. Frozen fries served in an air fryer contain just 2 grams of fat per serving, compared to 17 grams per serving of deep-fried equivalents. The precise number depends on the dish, but since not all recipes call for oil, we should eat a lot less of it.

Fried foods may be argued to be better than non-fried foods because they use less fat. Since you don't use too much oil at the start, they consume more fat from the air than fried foods, making them healthier.

Most people believe that using oil in a deep fryer to produce healthier meals is unnecessary, and that doing so will result in damp, dry, chewy food. In the breeze, what is used to fry food is normally really fine, so it is much easier than that. You can make all of the same foods in the microwave as you can in a regular microwave, such as burgers and fries.

If you prefer to make your own finger food, a deep fryer is a great way to bake things that you would normally make in the oven, such as cookies and cakes, and they taste so much better. It's too much fun to experiment with various kinds of cookies, cakes, and other sweets, and it's even practical to serve a range of individual desserts, such as ice cream, chocolate chips, and even biscuits.

You just need a computer if you want to roast bread or chicken wings. They're baked into a tasty crispy pastry in the well-insulated high-tech low-pressure fryer.

Deep fryers can cook a perfectly fried New York strip in under a minute, but they don't heat the kitchen the same way an oven does. Cooking times in the fryer are shorter than in traditional ovens, and this is due to their reduced size, which helps the food to flow more quickly and get cooler.
They may not be able to produce roasting-like cooking results, but that does not mean they aren't worth adding to your kitchen range. If you wish to purchase the unit, here are a few recipes that you can make at home with it. You will be shocked by how you use the deep fryer, and you may even incorporate some of your favorite recipes to make it taste

almost as good as fast food while becoming somewhat healthier.

BREAKFAST RECIPES

1. Baked apple breakfast oats

Preparation Time: 6 minutes

Cooking Time: 15 minutes

Servings:1

Ingredients:

- 1/3 cup vanilla greek yogurt
- 1/3 cup rolled oats
- 1 apple
- 1 tbsp. Peanut butter

Directions:

1. Preheat the air fryer oven to 350°f and press start.
2. Cut apples into chunks approximately 1/2-inch-thick.
3. Place apples in an oven-safe dish with some space between each chunk and sprinkle with cinnamon.
4. Bake in the oven for 12 minutes
5. Combine yogurt and oats in a bowl.
6. Remove the apples from the oven and combine it with the yogurt.

7. Top with peanut butter for a delicious and high-protein breakfast.

Nutrition: Calories 350, Fat 11.2 g, carbs 52.5 g, Protein 12.7 g.

2. Cheesy baked-egg toast

Preparation Time:7 minutes

Cooking Time: 10 minutes

Servings:4

Ingredients:

- 4 slices of wheat bread
- 4 eggs
- 1 cup shredded cheese
- 2 tbsp. Softened butter

Directions:

1. Preheat the air fryer oven to 350°f.
2. Place bread on a greased baking sheet
3. Use a spoon to push a square into the bread, creating a little bed for the egg.
4. Sprinkle salt and pepper over the bread and break one egg into each square.
5. Spread butter over each edge of the bread
6. Sprinkle 1/4 cup cheese over the buttered area.

7. Bake for 10 minutes or until the eggs are solid and the cheese is golden brown.

Nutrition: calories 297, fat 20.4 g, carbs 12.3 g, Protein 16.3 g.

3. Cheesy bagel sandwiches

Preparation Time:7 minutes

Cooking Time: 5 minutes

Servings:2

Ingredients:

- 2 bagels
- 4 tsp. Honey mustard
- 4 slices cooked honey ham
- 4 slices of swiss cheese

Directions:

1. Preheat the air fryer oven to 350°f.
2. Spread honey mustard on each half of the bagel
3. Add ham and cheese and close the bagel.
4. Bake the sandwich until the cheese is fully melted, approximately 5 minutes.

Nutrition: calories 588, fat 20.1 g, carbs 62.9 g, protein 38.4 g.

4. Peanut butter banana boats

Preparation Time:6 minutes

Cooking Time: 15 minutes

Servings:1

Ingredients:

- 1 banana
- 1/4 cup peanut butter
- 1/4 cup jelly
- 1 tbsp. Granola

Directions:

1. Preheat the air fryer oven to 350°f.
2. Slice the banana lengthwise and separate slightly.
3. Spread peanut butter and jelly in the gap
4. Sprinkle granola over the entire banana.
5. Bake for 15 minutes.

Nutrition: calories 724, fat 36.6 g, carbs 102.9 g, protein 20.0 g.

5. Avocado with poached eggs

Preparation Time:7 minutes

Cooking Time: 10 minutes

Servings:1

Ingredients:

- 2 eggs
- 1/2 avocado
- 2 slices bread
- 1 bunch spinach
- Pinch of salt
- Pinch of pepper

Directions:

1. Preheat the air fryer oven to 350°f.
2. Bring a pan of water to a boil.
3. Place bread on a pan and toast it in the oven for 10 minutes. Once the water is boiling, whisk it around in a circle.
4. Drop one egg in the hole and turn the heat to low, and then poach for 2 minutes.

5. Repeat with the second egg.
6. Mash avocado and spread it over the toast while the eggs poach.
7. Add the eggs to the toast and top with spinach.

Nutrition: calories 409, fat 29.7 g, carbs 21.7 g, protein 22.7 g.

BRUNCH RECIPES

6. Turkey burrito

Preparation Time: 10 minutes

Cooking Time: 10 minutes

Servings: 2

Ingredients:

- 4 slices turkey breast, cooked
- ½ red bell pepper, sliced
- 2 eggs
- 1 small avocado, peeled, pitted, and sliced
- 2 tablespoons salsa
- Salt and black pepper, to taste
- ⅛ cup mozzarella cheese, grated
- Tortillas for serving

Directions:

1. In a bowl, whisk the eggs with salt and pepper. Pour them in a pan and place in the air fryer's basket.
2. Cook at 400f for 5 minutes. Remove from the fryer and transfer eggs to a plate.
3. Arrange tortillas on a working surface. Divide eggs, turkey meat, bell pepper, cheese, salsa, and avocado between them.
4. Roll the burritos. Line the air fryer basket with tin foil and place the burritos inside.
5. Heat up the burritos at 300f for 3 minutes.

6. Serve.

Nutrition: calories: 349, fat: 23g, carb: 20g, protein: 21g

7. Breakfast bread pudding

Preparation Time: 10 minutes

Cooking Time: 22 minutes

Servings: 2

Ingredients:

- ¼ pound white bread, cubed
- 6 tablespoons milk
- 6 tablespoons water
- 1 teaspoon cornstarch
- ¼ cup apple, peeled, cored, and chopped
- 2 ½ tablespoons honey
- ½ teaspoon vanilla extract
- 1 teaspoon cinnamon powder
- ¾ cup flour
- ⅓ cup brown sugar
- 1 ½ ounces soft butter

Directions:

1. In a bowl, combine bread, apple, cornstarch, vanilla, cinnamon, honey, milk, and water. Whisk well.
2. In another bowl, combine butter, sugar, and flour and mix well.
3. Press half of the crumble mixture into the bottom of the air fryer, add bread and apple mixture, then add the rest of the crumble. Cook at 350f for 22 minutes.
4. Divide bread pudding onto plates and serve.

Nutrition: calories: 261 fat: 7g carb: 8g protein: 5g

LUNCH RECIPES

8. Ground chicken meatballs

Preparation Time: 10 minutes

Cooking Time: 10 minutes

Servings: 2

Ingredients

- 1-lb. Ground chicken
- 1/3 cup panko
- 1 teaspoon salt
- 2 teaspoons chives
- 1/2 teaspoon garlic powder
- 1 teaspoon thyme
- 1 egg

Directions:

1. Toss all the meatball ingredients in a bowl and mix well.
2. Make small meatballs out of this mixture and place them in the air fryer basket.
3. Press the "power button" of the air fry oven and turn the dial to select the "air fry" mode.
4. Press the time button and again turn the dial to set the cooking time to 10 minutes.
5. Now push the temp button and rotate the dial to set the temperature at 350 degrees f.

6. Once preheated, place the air fryer basket inside and close its lid.
7. Serve warm.

Nutrition: Calories 453 Total fat 2.4 g Saturated fat 3 g Cholesterol 21 mg Sodium 216 mg Total carbs 18 g Fiber 2.3 g Sugar 1.2 g Protein 23.2 g

9. Lamb potato chips baked

Preparation Time: 10 minutes

Cooking Time: 25 minutes

Servings: 2

Ingredients

- ½ lb. Minced lamb
- 1 tbs parsley chopped
- 2 teaspoon curry powder
- 1 pinch salt and black pepper
- 1 lb. Potato cooked, mashed
- 1 oz. Cheese grated
- 1 ½ oz. Potato chips crushed

Directions:

1. Mix lamb, curry powder, seasoning and parsley.
2. Spread this lamb mixture in a casserole dish.
3. Top the lamb mixture with potato mash, cheese, and potato chips.
4. Press "power button" of air fry oven and turn the dial to select the "bake" mode.
5. Press the time button and again turn the dial to set the cooking time to 20 minutes.
6. Now push the temp button and rotate the dial to set the temperature at 350 degrees f.
7. Once preheated, place casserole dish in the oven and close its lid.
8. Serve warm.

Nutrition: Calories 301 Total fat 15.8 g Saturated fat 2.7 g Cholesterol 75 mg Sodium 189 mg Total carbs 31.7 g Fiber 0.3 g Sugar 0.1 g Protein 28.2 g

10. Delicious creamy green beans

Preparation Time: 10 minutes

Cooking Time: 15 minutes

Servings: 2

Ingredients:

- ½ cup heavy cream
- 1 cup mozzarella, shredded
- 2/3 cup parmesan, grated
- Salt and black pepper to the taste
- 2 pounds green beans
- 2 teaspoons lemon zest, grated
- A pinch of red pepper flakes

Directions:

1. Put the beans in a dish that fits your air fryer, add heavy cream, salt, pepper, lemon zest, pepper flakes, mozzarella and parmesan, toss, introduce in your air fryer and cook at 350 degrees f for 15 minutes.
2. Divide among plates and serve right away.
3. Enjoy!

Nutrition: calories 231, fat 6, fiber 7, carbs 8, protein 5

DINNER RECIPES

11. Hummus and feta omelet

Preparation Time: 10 minutes

Cooking Time: 20 minutes

Servings: 1

Ingredients

- 1 large egg
- 2 large egg whites
- 1 tsp water
- Salt and pepper to taste
- 1 tbsp light butter
- 0.5 oz feta cheese
- 1 tbsp fresh, thinly sliced basil
- 2 tbsp diced tomatoes

Direction

1. In a mixing bowl, combine the egg, egg whites, water, salt and pepper and whisk together.
2. Add the butter. Make sure the butter coats the bottom of baking dish as it melts. Once the butter is melted, add the egg mixture to the baking dish and cook in air fryer for 5 mins.
3. Drop small amounts of hummus in the center of the omelet. Sprinkle feta over it and cook for 5 mins in air fryer.

4. When cooked, sprinkle the sliced basil and diced tomatoes over the top of the omelet and serve.

Nutrition: Carbs: 7g Fat: 19g Protein: 17g Fiber: 2g Sodium: 394mg

12. Chicken muffins

Preparation Time: 20 minutes

Cooking Time: 25 minutes

Servings: 16

Ingredients

- 1 ½ lbs. Chicken breast
- 1 egg
- 1 egg whites
- 6 tbsp dried breadcrumbs
- ¾ tsp dried basil
- ¾ tsp dried thyme
- ¾ tsp oregano
- 2 garlic cloves, minced
- ½ a small onion
- ¾ tsp salt
- 1/3 tsp black pepper
- ¾ cup parmesan cheese
- ¾ cup pasta sauce
- ¾ cup mozzarella cheese
- Oregano or basil for garnish

Direction

1. Preheat the air fryer to 350. Lightly mist a muffin tin with cooking spray and set aside.
2. In a large bowl, combine the ground chicken, egg, egg whites, breadcrumbs, basil, thyme, oregano, garlic, onion, salt, pepper and parmesan cheese and lightly mix together.

3. Form the meat mixture evenly into the 12 cups of your prepared muffin tin. Spread the pasta sauce evenly over the tops of each muffin. Bake for 20 minutes and remove from the fryer. Top each muffin with about a tbsp of shredded cheese and then return to the fryer for 2-3 minutes until the cheese is melted. Garnish.

Nutrition: Carbs: 6g Fat: 5g Protein: 18g Fiber: 0g Sodium: 121.8mg

13. Stuffed strawberries

Preparation Time: 10 minutes

Cooking Time: 10 minutes

Servings: 16

Ingredients

- 1 lb. Fresh strawberries
- 4 oz cream cheese
- ¼ cup powdered sugar
- ¼ tsp vanilla extract
- 1 full-sized low-fat graham cracker

Direction

1. Cut tops off strawberries.
2. Remove interior of each strawberry.
3. Cook it for 5 mins in air fryer.
4. Take a bowl, add cheese, sugar, vanilla and mix it in mixer.
5. Add this mixture inside strawberries.
6. Then coat the strawberries with crackers.
7. Enjoy.

Nutrition: Carbs: 5g Fat: 2g Protein: 1g Fiber: 0g Sodium: 33.7mg

DISH RECIPES

14. Coriander artichokes

Preparation Time: 20 minutes

Cooking Time: 10 minutes

Servings: 4

Ingredients:

- 12 oz. Artichoke hearts
- 1 tbsp. Lemon juice
- 1 tsp. Coriander, ground
- ½ tsp. Cumin seeds
- ½ tsp. Olive oil
- Salt and black pepper to taste.

Directions:

1. In a pan that fits your air fryer, mix all the ingredients, toss, introduce the pan in the fryer and cook at 370°f for 15 minutes
2. Divide the mix between plates and serve as a side dish.

Nutrition: calories: 200; fat: 7g; fiber: 2g; carbs: 5g; protein: 8g

15. Roasted eggplant

Preparation Time: 30 minutes

Cooking Time: 15 minutes

Servings: 4

Ingredients:

- 1 large eggplant
- 2 tbsp. Olive oil
- ½ tsp. Garlic powder.
- ¼ tsp. Salt

Directions:

1. Remove top and bottom from eggplant. Slice eggplant into ¼-inch-thick round slices.
2. Brush slices with olive oil.
3. Sprinkle with salt and garlic powder
4. Place eggplant slices into the air fryer basket.
5. Adjust the temperature to 390 degrees f and set the timer for 15 minutes.
6. Serve immediately.

Nutrition: calories: 91; protein: 1.3g; fiber: 3.7g; fat: 6.7g; carbs: 7.5g

16. Spinach dip

Preparation Time: 15 minutes

Cooking Time: 35 minutes

Servings: 8

Ingredients:

- 1 (8-oz. Package cream cheese, softened
- 1 cup mayonnaise
- 1 cup parmesan cheese, grated
- 1 cup frozen spinach, thawed and squeezed
- 1/3 cup water chestnuts, drained and chopped
- ½ cup onion, minced
- ¼ teaspoon garlic powder
- Ground black pepper, as required

Directions:

1. In a bowl, add all the ingredients and mix until well combined.
2. Transfer the mixture into a baking pan and spread in an even layer.
3. Press "power button" of air fry oven and turn the dial to select the "air fry" mode.
4. Press the time button and again turn the dial to set the cooking time to 35 minutes.
5. Now push the temp button and rotate the dial to set the temperature at 300 degrees f.
6. Press "start/pause" button to start.
7. When the unit beeps to show that it is preheated, open the lid.

8. Arrange pan over the "wire rack" and insert in the oven.
9. Stir the dip once halfway through.
10. Serve hot.

Nutrition: calories 258 total fat 22.1 g saturated fat 8.9 g cholesterol 47 mg sodium 384 mg total carbs 9.4 g fiber 0.3 g sugar 2.3 g protein 6.7 g

17. Spiced cauliflower

Preparation Time: 20 minutes

Cooking Time: 10 minutes

Servings: 4

Ingredients:

- 1 cauliflower head, florets separated
- 1 tbsp. Olive oil
- 1 tbsp. Butter; melted
- ¼ tsp. Cinnamon powder
- ¼ tsp. Cloves, ground
- ¼ tsp. Turmeric powder
- ½ tsp. Cumin, ground
- A pinch of salt and black pepper

Directions:

1. Take a bowl and mix cauliflower florets with the rest of the ingredients and toss.
2. Put the cauliflower in your air fryer's basket and cook at 390°f for 15 minutes
3. Divide between plates and serve as a side dish.

Nutrition: calories: 182; fat: 8g; fiber: 2g; carbs: 4g; protein: 8g

VEGETARIAN RECIPES

18. Protein: 15g Basil tomatoes

Preparation Time: 10 minutes

Cooking Time: 10 minutes

Servings: 2

Ingredients:

- 3 tomatoes, halved
- Olive oil cooking spray
- Salt and ground black pepper, as required
- 1 tablespoon fresh basil, chopped

Directions:

1. Drizzle cut sides of the tomato halves with cooking spray evenly.
2. Sprinkle with salt, black pepper and basil.
3. Press "power button" of air fry oven and turn the dial to select the "air fry" mode.
4. Press the time button and again turn the dial to set the cooking time to 10 minutes.
5. Now push the temp button and rotate the dial to set the temperature at 320 degrees f.
6. Press "start/pause" button to start.
7. When the unit beeps to show that it is preheated, open the lid.
8. Arrange the tomatoes in "air fry basket" and insert in the oven.

9. Serve warm.

Nutrition: Calories 34 Total fat 0.4 g Saturated fat 0.1 g Cholesterol 0 mg Sodium 87 mg Total carbs 7.2 g Fiber 2.2 g Sugar 4.9 g Protein 1.7 g

19. Pesto tomatoes

Preparation Time: 15 minutes

Cooking Time: 14 minutes

Servings: 4

Ingredients:

- 3 large heirloom tomatoes cut into ½ inch thick slices.
- 1 cup pesto
- 8 oz. Feta cheese cut into ½ inch thick slices.
- ½ cup red onions, sliced thinly
- 1 tablespoon olive oil

Directions:

1. Spread some pesto on each slice of tomato.
2. Top each tomato slice with a feta slice and onion and drizzle with oil.
3. Press "power button" of air fry oven and turn the dial to select the "air fry" mode.
4. Press the time button and again turn the dial to set the cooking time to 14 minutes.
5. Now push the temp button and rotate the dial to set the temperature at 390 degrees f.
6. Press "start/pause" button to start.
7. When the unit beeps to show that it is preheated, open the lid.
8. Arrange the tomatoes in greased "air fry basket" and insert in the oven.
9. Serve warm.

Nutrition: Calories 480 Total fat 41.9 g Saturated fat 14 g Cholesterol 65 mg Sodium 1000 mg Total carbs 13 g Fiber 3 g Sugar 10.5 g Protein 15.4 g

20. Stuffed tomatoes

Preparation Time: 15 minutes

Cooking Time: 15 minutes

Servings: 2

Ingredients:

- 2 large tomatoes
- ½ cup broccoli, chopped finely
- ½ cup cheddar cheese, shredded
- Salt and ground black pepper, as required
- 1 tablespoon unsalted butter, melted
- ½ teaspoon dried thyme, crushed

Directions:

1. Carefully, cut the top of each tomato and scoop out pulp and seeds.
2. In a bowl, mix together chopped broccoli, cheese, salt and black pepper.
3. Stuff each tomato with broccoli mixture evenly.
4. Press "power button" of air fry oven and turn the dial to select the "air fry" mode.
5. Press the time button and again turn the dial to set the cooking time to 15 minutes.
6. Now push the temp button and rotate the dial to set the temperature at 355 degrees f.
7. Press "start/pause" button to start.
8. When the unit beeps to show that it is preheated, open the lid.

9. Arrange the tomatoes in greased "air fry basket" and insert in the oven.

10. serve warm with the garnishing of thyme.

Nutrition: Calories 206 Total fat 15.6 g Saturated fat 9.7 g Cholesterol 45 mg Sodium 310 mg Total carbs 9 g Fiber 2.9 g Sugar 5.3 g Protein 9.4 g

21. Parmesan asparagus

Preparation Time: 10 minutes

Cooking Time: 10 minutes

Servings: 3

Ingredients:

- 1 lb. Fresh asparagus, trimmed
- 1 tablespoon parmesan cheese, grated
- 1 tablespoon butter, melted
- 1 teaspoon garlic powder
- Salt and ground black pepper, as required

Directions:

1. In a bowl, mix together the asparagus, cheese, butter, garlic powder, salt, and black pepper.
2. Press "power button" of air fry oven and turn the dial to select the "air fry" mode.
3. Press the time button and again turn the dial to set the cooking time to 10 minutes.
4. Now push the temp button and rotate the dial to set the temperature at 400 degrees f.
5. Press "start/pause" button to start.
6. When the unit beeps to show that it is preheated, open the lid.
7. Arrange the veggie mixture in greased "air fry basket" and insert in the oven.
8. Serve hot.

Nutrition: Calories 73 Total fat 4.4 g Saturated fat 2.7 g Cholesterol 12 mg Sodium 95 mg Total carbs 6.6 g Fiber 3.3 g Sugar 3.1 g Protein 4.2 g

22. Almond asparagus

Preparation Time: 15 minutes

Cooking Time: 6 minutes

Servings: 3

Ingredients:

- 1 lb. Asparagus
- 2 tablespoons olive oil
- 2 tablespoons balsamic vinegar
- Salt and ground black pepper, as required
- 1/3 cup almonds, sliced

Directions:

1. In a bowl, mix together the asparagus, oil, vinegar, salt, and black pepper.
2. Press "power button" of air fry oven and turn the dial to select the "air fry" mode.
3. Press the time button and again turn the dial to set the cooking time to 6minutes.
4. Now push the temp button and rotate the dial to set the temperature at 400 degrees f.
5. Press "start/pause" button to start.
6. When the unit beeps to show that it is preheated, open the lid.
7. Arrange the veggie mixture in greased "air fry basket" and insert in the oven.
8. Serve hot.

Nutrition: Calories 173 Total fat 14.8 g Saturated fat 1.8 g Cholesterol 0 mg Sodium 54 mg Total carbs 8.2 g Fiber 4.5 g Sugar 3.3 g Protein 5.6 g

23. Spicy butternut squash

Preparation Time: 15 minutes

Cooking Time: 20 minutes

Servings: 4

Ingredients:

- 1 medium butternut squash, peeled, seeded and cut into chunk
- 2 teaspoons cumin seeds
- 1/8 teaspoon garlic powder
- 1/8 teaspoon chili flakes, crushed
- Salt and ground black pepper, as required
- 1 tablespoon olive oil
- 2 tablespoons pine nuts
- 2 tablespoons fresh cilantro, chopped

Directions:

1. In a bowl, mix together the squash, spices, and oil.
2. Press "power button" of air fry oven and turn the dial to select the "air fry" mode.
3. Press the time button and again turn the dial to set the cooking time to 20 minutes.
4. Now push the temp button and rotate the dial to set the temperature at 375 degrees f.
5. Press "start/pause" button to start.
6. When the unit beeps to show that it is preheated, open the lid.
7. Arrange the squash chunks in greased "air fry basket" and insert in the oven.

8. Serve hot with the garnishing of pine nuts and cilantro.

Nutrition: Calories 191 Total fat 7 g Saturated fat 0.8 g Cholesterol 0 mg Sodium 52 mg Total carbs 34.3 g Fiber 6 g Sugar 6.4 g Protein 3.7 g

24. Caramelized baby carrots

Preparation Time: 10 minutes

Cooking Time: 15 minutes

Servings: 4

Ingredients:

- ½ cup butter, melted
- ½ cup brown sugar
- 1 lb. Bag baby carrots

Directions:

1. In a bowl, mix together the butter, brown sugar and carrots.
2. Press "power button" of air fry oven and turn the dial to select the "air fry" mode.
3. Press the time button and again turn the dial to set the cooking time to 15 minutes.
4. Now push the temp button and rotate the dial to set the temperature at 400 degrees f.
5. Press "start/pause" button to start.
6. When the unit beeps to show that it is preheated, open the lid.
7. Arrange the carrots in greased "air fry basket" and insert in the oven.
8. Serve warm.

Nutrition: Calories 312 Total fat 23.2 g Saturated fat 14.5 g Cholesterol 61 mg Sodium 257 mg Total carbs 27.1 g Fiber 3.3 g Sugar 23 g Protein 1 g

25. Broccoli with cauliflower

Preparation Time: 15 minutes

Cooking Time: 20 minutes

Servings: 4

Ingredients:

- 1½ cups broccoli, cut into 1-inch pieces
- 1½ cups cauliflower, cut into 1-inch pieces
- 1 tablespoon olive oil
- Salt, as required

Directions:

1. In a bowl, add the vegetables, oil, and salt and toss to coat well.
2. Press "power button" of air fry oven and turn the dial to select the "air fry" mode.
3. Press the time button and again turn the dial to set the cooking time to 20 minutes.
4. Now push the temp button and rotate the dial to set the temperature at 375 degrees f.
5. Press "start/pause" button to start.
6. When the unit beeps to show that it is preheated, open the lid.
7. Arrange the veggie mixture in greased "air fry basket" and insert in the oven.
8. Serve hot.

Nutrition: Calories 51 Total fat 3.7 g Saturated fat 0.5 g Cholesterol 0 mg Sodium 61 mg Total carbs 4.3 g Fiber 1.8 g Sugar 1.5 g Protein 1.7 g

26. Cauliflower in buffalo sauce

Preparation Time: 13 minutes

Cooking Time: 12 minutes

Servings: 4

Ingredients:

- 1 large head cauliflower, cut into bite-size florets
- 1 tablespoon olive oil
- 2 teaspoons garlic powder
- Salt and ground black pepper, as required
- 1 tablespoon butter, melted
- 2/3 cup warm buffalo sauce

Directions:

1. In a large bowl, add cauliflower florets, olive oil, garlic powder, salt and pepper and toss to coat.
2. Press "power button" of air fry oven and turn the dial to select the "air fry" mode.
3. Press the time button and again turn the dial to set the cooking time to 12 minutes.
4. Now push the temp button and rotate the dial to set the temperature at 375 degrees f.
5. Press "start/pause" button to start.
6. When the unit beeps to show that it is preheated, open the lid.
7. Arrange the cauliflower florets in "air fry basket" and insert in the oven.
8. After 7 minutes of cooking, coat the cauliflower florets with buffalo sauce.

9. Serve hot.

Nutrition: Calories 183 Total fat 17.1 g Saturated fat 4.3 g Cholesterol 8 mg Sodium 826 mg Total carbs 5.9 g Fiber 1.8 g Sugar 1.9 g Protein 1.6 g

POULTRY RECIPES

27. Tasty turkey burgers recipe

Preparation Time: 0 minutes + **Cooking Time:** 18 minutes

Servings: 4

Ingredients:

- Turkey meat - 1 lb.; ground
- Shallot - 1; minced
- A drizzle of olive oil
- Small jalapeno pepper - 1; minced
- Lime juice - 2 tsp.
- Lime zest – 1; grated
- Cumin - 1 tsp.; ground
- Sweet paprika - 1 tsp.
- Salt and black pepper to the taste
- Guacamole for serving

Directions:

1. Mix turkey meat with salt, pepper, cumin, paprika, shallot, jalapeno, lime juice and zest in a clean bowl.
2. Stir gently and shape burgers from this mix.
3. Drizzle the oil over the burgers.
4. Move to the preheated air fryer and cook them at a temperature of 370 °f for 8 minutes on each side.
5. Divide into different
6. Serve with guacamole as toppings.

Nutrition: Calories: 200; fat: 12; fiber: 0; carbs: 0; protein: 12

28. Special coconut creamy chicken

Preparation Time: 0 minutes

Cooking Time: 2 hours 25 minutes

Servings: 4

Ingredients:

- Big chicken legs 4
- Salt and black pepper to the taste
- Grated ginger; -2 tbsp.
- Coconut cream-4 tbsp.
- Turmeric powder-5 tsp.

Directions:

1. Mix the cream with turmeric, ginger, salt, and pepper, in a bowl; whisk and include chicken pieces, hurl them well and put aside for 2 hours.
2. Move chicken to your preheated air fryer, cook at 370 °f, for 25 minutes;
3. Share meal between plates and present with a side serving of mixed greens.

Nutrition: Calories: 300; fat: 4; fiber: 12; protein: 20; carbs: 22;

29. Duck with cherries recipe

Preparation Time: 0 minutes

Cooking Time: 30 minutes

Servings: 4

Ingredients:

- Duck breasts; boneless, skin on and scored-4
- Ginger; grated-1 tbsp.
- Rhubarb; sliced-2 cups
- Salt and black pepper to the taste
- Ground cumin-1 tsp.
- Minced garlic-1 tsp.
- Pitted cherries-2 cups
- Sugar 1/2 cup
- Ground clove 1/2 tsp.
- Honey 1/4 cup
- Chopped yellow onion 1/2 cup
- Cinnamon powder 1/2 tsp.
- Balsamic vinegar 1/3 cup
- Chopped sage leaves 4
- Chopped
- Jalapeno 1

Directions:

1. Start by spicing the duck bosom with salt and pepper, put in your air fryer preheated to 350 °f, and cook for 5 minutes on each side.
2. On the other hand; heat a dish to over medium warmth, include sugar, nectar, vinegar, garlic, ginger,

cumin, clove, cinnamon, sage, jalapeno, rhubarb, onion, and fruits; blend appropriately, at that point bring to a stew and cook for 10 minutes.

3. Add duck bosoms and hurl well,
4. Share everything among plates and serve.

Nutrition: Calories: 456; fiber: 4; fat: 13; protein: 31; carbs: 64;

30. Quick and easy duck breasts recipe

Preparation Time: 0 minutes

Cooking Time: 25 minutes

Servings: 4

Ingredients:

1. Skinless and boneless-4 duck breasts
2. Lemon juice-2 tbsp.
3. Salt and black pepper to the taste
4. Lemon pepper 1/2 tsp.
5. Garlic heads; peeled, tops cut off and quartered-4
6. Olive oil-1 ½ tbsp.

Directions:

1. Mix duck bosoms with garlic, lemon juice, salt, pepper, lemon pepper and olive oil in a bowl and hurl everything appropriately.
2. Move the duck and garlic to your air fryer and cook at 350 °f, for 15 minutes.
3. Share duck bosoms and garlic among plates and serve.

Nutrition: Calories: 200; fiber: 1; fat: 7; carbs: 11; protein: 17

31. Duck and tea sauce recipe

Preparation Time: 0 minutes

Cooking Time: 30 minutes

Servings: 2

Ingredients:

- Duck breast halves; boneless-2
- Chopped shallot 3/4 cup
- Salt and black pepper to the taste
- Chicken stock-2 ¼ cup
- Orange juice-1 ½ cup
- Earl gray tea leaves-3 tsp.
- Melted butter-3 tbsp.
- Honey-1 tbsp.

Directions:

1. Season duck bosom parts with salt and pepper, move to your preheated air fryer and cook at 360 °f, for 10 minutes.
2. On the other hand; heat a skillet with the margarine to over medium warmth, include shallot; mix and cook for 2-3 minutes.
3. Include stock; mix and cook for one more moment.
4. Include squeezed orange, tea leaves, and nectar; mix, cook for 2-3 minutes more and strain into a bowl.
5. Share duck on plates; spread tea sauce all finished and serve.

Nutrition: Calories: 228; fiber: 2; fat: 11; protein: 12; carbs: 20;

SEAFOOD RECIPES

32. Lime baked salmon

Preparation Time: 22 minutes

Cooking Time: 12 minutes

Servings: 2

Ingredients:

- 2 (3-oz. Salmon fillets, skin removed
- ¼ cup sliced pickled jalapeños
- ½ medium lime, juiced
- 2 tbsp. Chopped cilantro
- 1 tbsp. Salted butter; melted.
- ½ tsp. Finely minced garlic
- 1 tsp. Chili powder

Directions:

1. Place salmon fillets into a 6-inch round baking pan. Brush each with butter and sprinkle with chili powder and garlic
2. Place jalapeño slices on top and around salmon. Pour half of the lime juice over the salmon and cover with foil. Place pan into the air fryer basket. Adjust the temperature to 370 degrees f and set the timer for 12 minutes
3. When fully cooked, salmon should flake easily with a fork and reach an internal temperature of at least 145 degrees f.

4. To serve, spritz with remaining lime juice and garnish with cilantro.

Nutrition: Calories: 167 Protein: 18g Fiber: 7g Fat: 9g Carbs: 6g

33. Sea bass and fennel

Preparation Time: 25 minutes

Cooking Time: 20 minutes

Servings: 2

Ingredients:

- ¼ cup black olives, pitted and sliced
- 2 sea bass, fillets
- ¼ cup basil; chopped.
- 1 fennel bulb; sliced
- Juice of 1 lemon
- 1 tbsp. Olive oil
- A pinch of salt and black pepper

Directions:

1. In a pan that fits the air fryer, combine all the ingredients.
2. Introduce the pan in the machine and cook at 380°f for 20 minutes, shaking the fryer halfway.
3. Divide between plates and serve

Nutrition: Calories: 254 Fat: 10g Fiber: 4g Carbs: 6g Protein: 11g

34. Snapper and spring onions

Preparation Time: 19 minutes

Cooking Time: 14 minutes

Servings: 4

Ingredients:

- 4 snapper fillets; boneless and skin scored
- 6 spring onions; chopped.
- Juice of ½ lemon
- 3 tbsp. Olive oil
- 2 tbsp. Sweet paprika
- A pinch of salt and black pepper

Directions:

1. Take a bowl and mix the paprika with the rest of the **ingredients:** except the fish and whisk well
2. Rub the fish with this mix, place the fillets in your air fryer's basket and cook at 390°f for 7 minutes on each side.
3. Divide between plates and serve with a side salad.

Nutrition: Calories: 241 Fat: 12g Fiber: 4g Carbs: 6g Protein: 13g

35. Herbed trout and asparagus

Preparation Time: 25 minutes

Cooking Time: 14 minutes

Servings: 4

Ingredients:

- 4 trout fillets; boneless and skinless
- 1 bunch asparagus; trimmed
- ¼ cup mixed chives and tarragon
- 2 tbsp. Ghee; melted
- 2 tbsp. Olive oil
- 1 tbsp. Lemon juice
- A pinch of salt and black pepper

Directions:

1. Mix the asparagus with half of the oil, salt and pepper, put it in your air fryer's basket, cook at 380°f for 6 minutes and divide between plates
2. Take a bowl and mix the trout with salt, pepper, lemon juice, the rest of the oil and the herbs and toss,
3. Put the fillets in your air fryer's basket and cook at 380°f for 7 minutes on each side
4. Divide the fish next to the asparagus, drizzle the melted ghee all over and serve

Nutrition: Calories: 240 Fat: 12g Fiber: 4g Carbs: 6g Protein: 9g

36. Shrimp and zucchinis

Preparation Time: 20 minutes

Cooking Time: 15 minutes

Servings: 4

Ingredients:

- 1 lb. Shrimp; peeled and deveined
- 2 zucchinis; cut into medium cubes
- 1 tbsp. Lemon juice
- 1 tbsp. Olive oil
- 1 tbsp. Garlic; minced
- A pinch of salt and black pepper

Directions:

1. In a pan that fits the air fryer, combine all the ingredients, toss, put the pan in the machine and cook at 370°f for 15 minutes.
2. Divide between plates and serve right away

Nutrition: Calories: 221 Fat: 9g Fiber: 2g Carbs: 15g Protein: 11g

MEAT RECIPES

37. Crispy fried pork chops the southern way

Preparation Time: 10 minutes

Cooking Time: 25 minutes

Servings: 4

Ingredients:

- ½ cup all-purpose flour
- ½ cup low fat buttermilk
- ½ teaspoon black pepper
- ½ teaspoon tabasco sauce
- Teaspoon paprika
- 3 bone-in pork chops

Directions:

1. Place the buttermilk and hot sauce in a ziploc bag and add the pork chops. Allow to marinate for at least an hour in the fridge.
2. In a bowl, combine the flour, paprika, and black pepper.
3. Remove pork from the ziploc bag and dredge in the flour mixture.
4. Preheat the air fryer oven to 390°f.
5. Spray the pork chops with cooking oil.

6. Pour into the oven rack/basket. Place the rack on the middle-shelf of the air fryer oven. Set temperature to 390°f and set time to 25 minutes.

Nutrition: calories: 427; fat: 21.2g; protein:46.4g; sugar:2g

38. Cilantro-mint pork bbq thai style

Preparation Time: 5 minutes

Cooking Time: 15 minutes

Servings: 3

Ingredients:

- 1 minced hot chili
- 1 minced shallot
- 1-pound ground pork
- 2 tablespoons fish sauce
- 2 tablespoons lime juice
- 3 tablespoons basil
- Tablespoons chopped mint
- 3 tablespoons cilantro

Directions:

1. In a shallow dish, mix well all ingredients with hands. Form into 1-inch ovals.
2. Thread ovals in skewers. Place on skewer rack in air fryer.
3. For 15 minutes, cook on 360°f. Halfway through cooking time, turnover skewers. If needed, cook in batches.
4. Serve and enjoy.

Nutrition: calories: 455; fat: 31.5g; protein:40.4g

39. Tuscan pork chops

Preparation Time: 10 minutes

Cooking Time: 10 minutes

Servings: 4

Ingredients:

- 1/4 cup all-purpose flour
- 1 teaspoon salt
- 3/4 teaspoons seasoned pepper
- 4 (1-inch-thick) boneless pork chops
- 1 tablespoon olive oil
- 3 to 4 garlic cloves
- 1/3 cup balsamic vinegar
- 1/3 cup chicken broth
- 3 plum tomatoes, seeded and diced
- Tablespoons capers

Directions:

1. Combine flour, salt, and pepper
2. Press pork chops into flour mixture on both sides until evenly covered.
3. Cook in your air fryer oven at 360 degrees for 14 minutes, flipping halfway through.
4. While the pork chops cook, warm olive oil in a medium skillet.
5. Add garlic and sauté for 1 minute; then mix in vinegar and chicken broth.
6. Add capers and tomatoes and turn to high heat.

7. Bring the sauce to a boil, stirring regularly, then add pork chops, cooking for one minute.
8. Remove from heat and cover for about 5 minutes to allow the pork to absorb some of the sauce; serve hot.

Nutrition: calories: 349; fat: 23g; protein:20g; fiber:1.5g

40. Italian parmesan breaded pork chops

Preparation Time: 5 minutes

Cooking Time: 25 minutes

Servings: 5

Ingredients:

- 5 (3½- to 5-ounce) pork chops (bone-in or boneless)
- 1 teaspoon italian seasoning
- Seasoning salt
- Pepper
- ¼ cup all-purpose flour
- 2 tablespoons italian breadcrumbs
- 3 tablespoons finely grated parmesan cheese
- Cooking oil

Directions:

1. Season the pork chops with the italian seasoning and seasoning salt and pepper to taste.
2. Sprinkle the flour on both sides of the pork chops, then coat both sides with the breadcrumbs and parmesan cheese.
3. Place the pork chops in the air fryer basket. Stacking them is okay. Spray the pork chops with cooking oil. Set temperature to 390°f and cook for 6 minutes.
4. Open the air fryer and flip the pork chops. Cook for an additional 6 minutes.
5. Cool before serving. Instead of seasoning salt, you can use either chicken or pork rub for additional flavor.

You can find these rubs in the spice aisle of the grocery store.

Nutrition: calories: 334; fat: 7g; protein:34g; fiber:0g

DESSERT RECIPES

41. Pumpkin cookies

Preparation Time: 10 minutes

Cooking Time: 15 minutes

Servings: 24

Ingredients:

- 2 and ½ cups flour
- ½ teaspoon baking soda
- 1 tablespoon flax seed, ground
- 3 tablespoons water
- ½ cup pumpkin flesh, mashed
- ¼ cup honey
- 2 tablespoons butter
- 1 teaspoon vanilla extract
- ½ cup dark chocolate chips

Directions:

1. In a bowl, mix flax seed with water, stir and leave aside for a few minutes.
2. In another bowl, mix flour with salt and baking soda.
3. In a third bowl, mix honey with pumpkin puree, butter, vanilla extract and flaxseed.
4. Combine flour with honey mix and chocolate chips and stir.
5. Scoop 1 tablespoon of cookie dough on a lined baking sheet that fits your air fryer, repeat with the rest of the

dough, introduce them in your air fryer and cook at 350 degrees f for 15 minutes.

6. Leave cookies to cool down and serve.
7. Enjoy!

Nutrition: calories 140, fat 2, fiber 2, carbs 7, protein 10

42. Figs and coconut butter mix

Preparation Time: 6 minutes

Cooking Time: 4 minutes

Servings: 3

Ingredients:

- 2 tablespoons coconut butter
- 12 figs, halved
- ¼ cup sugar
- 1 cup almonds, toasted and chopped

Directions:

1. Put butter in a pan that fits your air fryer and melt over medium high heat.
2. Add figs, sugar and almonds, toss, introduce in your air fryer and cook at 300 degrees f for 4 minutes.
3. Divide into bowls and serve cold.
4. Enjoy!

Nutrition: calories 170, fat 4, fiber 5, carbs 7, protein 9

43. Lemon bars

Preparation Time: 10 minutes

Cooking Time: 25 minutes

Servings: 6

Ingredients:

- 4 eggs
- 2 and ¼ cups flour
- Juice from 2 lemons
- 1 cup butter, soft
- 2 cups sugar

Directions:

1. In a bowl, mix butter with ½ cup sugar and 2 cups flour, stir well, press on the bottom of a pan that fits your air fryer, introduce in the fryer and cook at 350 degrees f for 10 minutes.
2. In another bowl, mix the rest of the sugar with the rest of the flour, eggs and lemon juice, whisk well and spread over crust.
3. Introduce in the fryer at 350 degrees f for 15 minutes more, leave aside to cool down, cut bars and serve them.
4. Enjoy!

Nutrition: calories 125, fat 4, fiber 4, carbs 16, protein 2

APPETIZERS

44. Smoky Air Fried Asparagus with Sesame Seeds

Preparation Time: 5 minutes

Cooking Time: 10 minutes

Servings: 3

Ingredients:

- 8 ounces Asparagus spears, trimmed and halved crosswise
- Garnishing Ingredients
- 1 teaspoon smoked paprika
- 2 teaspoons sesame seeds
- Seasoning Ingredients
- 1 teaspoon peanut oil
- 1/2 teaspoon salt
- 1/2 teaspoon ground black pepper

Directions:

1. Preheat your air fryer to 350 degrees F.
2. Combine the seasoning ingredients thoroughly.
3. Add the vegetables and toss to coat.
4. Place in the basket of the air fryer and fry for 5 minutes
5. Shake and cook for another 5 minutes
6. Sprinkle with garnishing ingredients.

Nutrition: Calories 287 Fat 11 Carbs 25 Protein 30

SNACKS RECIPES

45. Fried Ravioli

Preparation Time: 15 minutes

Cooking Time: 8 minutes

Servings: 4

Ingredients:

- ½ cup panko breadcrumbs
- Salt and pepper to taste
- 1 teaspoon garlic powder
- 1 teaspoon dried oregano
- 1 teaspoon dried basil
- 2 teaspoons nutritional yeast flakes
- ¼ cup Aquafina liquid
- 8 oz. frozen vegan ravioli
- Cooking spray
- ½ cup marinara sauce

Directions:

1. Mix the breadcrumbs, salt, pepper, garlic powder, oregano, basil and nutritional yeast flakes on a plate.
2. In another bowl, pour the aquafaba liquid.
3. Dip each ravioli into the liquid and then coat with the breadcrumb mixture.
4. Put the ravioli in the air fryer.
5. Spray oil on the raviolis.
6. Cook at 390 degrees F for 6 minutes.

7. Flip each one and cook for another 2 minutes.

8. Serve with marinara sauce.

Nutrition: Calories 154 Total Fat 3.8g Saturated Fat 0.6g Cholesterol 7mg Sodium 169mg Total Carbohydrate 18.4g Dietary Fiber 1.5g Total Sugars 3g Protein 4.6g Potassium 154mg

46. Corn Fritters

Preparation Time: 15 minutes

Cooking Time: 10 minutes

Servings: 4

Ingredients:

- ¼ cup ground cornmeal
- ¼ cup flour
- Salt and pepper to taste
- ½ teaspoon baking powder
- ¼ teaspoon garlic powder
- ¼ teaspoon onion powder
- ¼ teaspoon paprika
- ¼ cup parsley, chopped
- 1 cup corn kernels mixed with 3 tablespoons almond milk
- 2 cups fresh corn kernels
- 4 tablespoons vegan mayonnaise
- 2 teaspoons grainy mustard

Directions:

1. Mix the cornmeal, flour, salt, pepper, baking powder, garlic powder, onion powder, paprika and parsley in a bowl.
2. Put the corn kernels with almond milk in a food processor.
3. Season with salt and pepper.
4. Pulse until well blended.
5. Add the corn kernels.

6. Transfer to a bowl and stir into the cornmeal mixture.
7. Pour a small amount of the batter in the air fryer pan.
8. Pour another a few centimeters away from the first fritter.
9. Cook in the air fryer at 350 degrees for 10 minutes or until golden.
10. Flip halfway through.
11. Serve with mayo mustard dip.

Nutrition: Calories 135 Total Fat 4.6g Saturated Fat 0.2g Cholesterol 0mg Sodium 136mg Carbohydrate 22.5g Dietary Fiber 2.5g

Total Sugars 2.7g Protein 3.5g   Potassium 308mg

47. Mushroom Pizza

Preparation Time: 15 minutes

Cooking Time: 10 minutes

Servings: 4

Ingredients:

- 4 large Portobello mushrooms, stems and gills removed
- 1 teaspoon balsamic vinegar
- Salt and pepper to taste
- 4 tablespoons vegan pasta sauce
- 1 clove garlic, minced
- 3 oz. zucchini, chopped
- 4 olives, sliced
- 2 tablespoons sweet red pepper, diced
- 1 teaspoon dried basil
- ½ cups hummus
- Fresh basil, minced

Directions:

1. Coat the mushrooms with balsamic vinegar and season with salt and pepper.
2. Spread pasta sauce inside each mushroom.
3. Sprinkle with minced garlic.
4. Preheat your air fryer to 330 degrees F.
5. Cook mushrooms for 3 minutes.
6. Take the mushrooms out and top with zucchini, olives, and peppers.
7. Season with salt, pepper and basil.

8. Put them back to the air fryer and cook for another 3 minutes.
9. Serve mushroom pizza with hummus and fresh basil.

Nutrition: Calories 70 Total Fat 1.56g Saturated Fat 0.5g Cholesterol 12 mg Sodium 167 mg Total Carbohydrate 11g Dietary Fiber 3.4g Total Sugars 3.8g Protein 4.3g Potassium 350 mg

OTHERS RECIPES

48. Taco Dogs

Preparation Time: 10 minutes

Cooking Time: 17 minutes

Servings: 2

Ingredients:

- 2 jumbo hot dogs
- 1 tsp taco seasoning mix
- 2 hot dog buns
- 1/3 cup guacamole
- 4 tbsp. salsa
- 6 pickled jalapeno slices

Directions:

1. Ensure that your air fryer is preheated at 390 F for at least four minutes.
2. Make five slits into each hot dog, and rub ½ teaspoon taco seasoning over each hot dog.
3. Allow the hot dogs to cook in the air fryer for about 5 minutes, before placing them in bus and back into the air fryer basket.
4. This time around, cook until the buns are toasted and hot dogs crisp. This takes about 4 minutes or more.
5. Top the hot dogs with guacamole, salsa, and jalapenos - all in equal amounts.

Nutrition: calories 343, fat 3, fiber 12, carbs 20, protein 26

49. Pizza Dogs

Preparation Time: 10 minutes

Cooking Time: 17 minutes

Servings: 2

Ingredients:

- 2 hot dogs
- 4 slices pepperoni, halved
- ½ cup pizza sauce
- 2 hot dog buns
- ¼ cup shredded mozzarella cheese
- 2 tsp sliced olives

Directions:

1. Ensure that your air fryer is preheated to 390 F.
2. Cut four slits into each hot dog, and place them into the basket of the air fryer.
3. Allow cooking for 3 minutes before withdrawing onto a cutting board using tongs.
4. Put a pepperoni half in each of the slits in the hot dogs. Divide the pizza sauce between the buns, and fill with the olives, hot dogs, and mozzarella cheese.
5. Place the hot dogs in the basket of the air fryer and allow to cook, again.
6. Remove when the cheese is melted, and the buns appear crisp - this takes about 2 minutes.

Nutrition: calories 156, fat 2, fiber 19, carbs 14, protein 28

50. Honey ginger salmon steaks

Preparation Time: 0 minutes

Cooking Time: 10 minutes

Servings: 2

Ingredients:

- 2 salmon steaks
- 2 tablespoons fresh ginger, minced
- 2 garlic cloves, minced
- ¼ cup honey
- 1/3 cup orange juice
- 1/3 cup soy sauce
- 1 lemon, sliced

Directions:

1. Mix all the ingredients in a bowl. Marinate the salmon in the sauce for 2-hours in the fridge. Add the marinated salmon to air fryer at 395°fahrenheit for 10-minutes. Garnish with fresh ginger and lemon slices.

Nutrition: calories: 514, total fat: 22g, carbs: 39.5g, protein: 41g

PIZZA, BREAD, WRAPS AND SANDWICHES

51. Cheesy Shrimp Sandwich

Preapration Time:10 minutes

Cooking Time: 5 to 7 minutes

Servings: 4

Ingredients:

- 1¼ cups shredded Colby, Cheddar, or Havarti cheese
- 1 (6-ounce / 170-g) can tiny shrimp, drained
- 3tablespoons mayonnaise
- 2tablespoons minced green onion
- 4slices whole grain or whole-wheat bread
- 2tablespoons softened butter

Directions:

1. In a medium bowl, combine the cheese, shrimp, mayonnaise, and green onion, and mix well.
2. Spread this mixture on two of the slices of bread. Top with the other slices of bread to make two sandwiches. Spread the sandwiches lightly with butter.
3. Select the Air Fry function and cook at 400 degrees Fahrenheit (204 degrees Celsius) for 5 to 7 minutes, or until the bread is browned and crisp and the cheese is melted.
4. Cut in half and serve warm.

Nutrition: Calories 602 Fat 23.9g Carbohydrates 46.5g Sugar 2.9g Protein 11.3g Sodium 886mg

52. Smoky Chicken Sandwich

Preapration Time:10 minutes

Cooking Time: 11 minutes

Servings: 2

Ingredients:

- 2boneless, skinless chicken breasts (8 ounces / 227 g each), sliced horizontally in half and separated into 4 thinner cutlets
- Kosher salt and freshly ground black pepper, to taste
- ½ cup all-purpose flour
- 3large eggs, lightly beaten
- ½ cup dried bread crumbs
- 1 tablespoon smoked paprika
- Cooking spray
- ½ cup marinara sauce
- 6ounces (170 g) smoked Mozzarella cheese, grated
- 2store-bought soft, sesame-seed hamburger or Italian buns, split

Directions:

1. Season the chicken cutlets all over with salt and pepper. Set up three shallow bowls: Place the flour in the first bowl, the eggs in the second, and stir together the bread crumbs and smoked paprika in the third. Coat the chicken pieces in the flour, then dip fully in the egg. Dredge in the paprika bread crumbs, then transfer to a wire rack set over a baking sheet and spray both sides liberally with cooking spray.

2. Transfer 2 of the chicken cutlets to the air fryer oven. Select the Air Fry function and cook at 350 degrees Fahrenheit (177 degrees Celsius) for 6 minutes, or until beginning to brown.

Spread each cutlet with 2 tablespoons of the marinara sauce and sprinkle with one-quarter of the smoked Mozzarella.

3. Increase the temperature to 400 degrees Fahrenheit (204 degrees Celsius) and air fry for 5 minutes more, or until the chicken is cooked through and crisp and the cheese is melted and golden brown.

4. Transfer the cutlets to a plate, stack on top of each other, and place inside a bun. Repeat with the remaining chicken cutlets, marinara, smoked Mozzarella, and bun.

5. Serve the sandwiches warm.

Nutrition: Calories 311 Fat 11g Carbohydrate 22g Protein 31g

53. Nugget and Veggie Taco Wraps

Preapration Time:5 minutes

Cooking Time: 15 minutes

Servings: 4

Ingredients:
- 1 tablespoon water
- 4pieces commercial vegan nuggets, chopped
- 1 small yellow onion, diced
- 1 small red bell pepper, chopped
- 2cobs grilled corn kernels
- 4large corn tortillas
- Mixed greens, for garnish

Directions:
1. Over a medium heat, sauté the nuggets in the water with the onion, corn kernels and bell pepper in a skillet, then remove from the heat.
2. Fill the tortillas with the nuggets and vegetables and fold them up. Transfer to the air fryer basket. Select the Air Fry function and cook at 400 degrees Fahrenheit (204 degrees Celsius) for 15 minutes.
3. Once crispy, serve immediately, garnished with the mixed greens.

Nutrition: Calories 140 Fat 4g Fiber 3g Carbohydrates 5g Protein 7g

54. Cheesy Greens Sandwich

Preapration Time:15 minutes

Cooking Time: 10 to 13 minutes

Servings: 4

Ingredients:

- 1½ cups chopped mixed greens
- 2garlic cloves, thinly sliced
- 2teaspoons olive oil
- 2slices low-sodium low-fat Swiss cheese
- 4slices low-sodium whole-wheat bread
- Cooking spray

Directions:

1. Select the Bake function and preheat Maxx to 400 degrees Fahrenheit (204 degrees Celsius).
2. In a baking pan, mix the greens, garlic, and olive oil. Bake for 4 to 5 minutes, stirring once, until the vegetables are tender. Drain, if necessary.
3. Make 2 sandwiches, dividing half of the greens and 1 slice of Swiss cheese between 2 slices of bread. Lightly spray the outsides of the sandwiches with cooking spray.
4. Bake the sandwiches in the air fryer oven for 6 to 8 minutes, turning with tongs halfway through, until the bread is toasted and the cheese melts.
5. Cut each sandwich in half and serve.

Nutrition:Calories 140 Fat 4g Fiber 3g Carbohydrates 5g Protein 7g

55. Cheesy Chicken Sandwich

Preapration Time:10 minutes

Cooking Time: 5 to 7 minutes

Servings: 1

Ingredients:

- ⅓ cup chicken, cooked and shredded
- 2Mozzarella slices
- 1 hamburger bun
- ¼ cup shredded cabbage
- 1 teaspoon mayonnaise
- 2teaspoons butter, melted
- 1 teaspoon olive oil
- ½ teaspoon balsamic vinegar
- ¼ teaspoon smoked paprika
- ¼ teaspoon black pepper
- ¼ teaspoon garlic powder
- Pinch of salt

Directions:

1. Select the Bake function and preheat Maxx to 370 degrees Fahrenheit (188 degrees Celsius).
2. Brush some butter onto the outside of the hamburger bun.
3. In a bowl, coat the chicken with the garlic powder, salt, pepper, and paprika.
4. In a separate bowl, stir together the mayonnaise, olive oil, cabbage, and balsamic vinegar to make coleslaw.
5. Slice the bun in two. Start building the sandwich, starting with the chicken, followed by the Mozzarella, the coleslaw, and finally the top bun.

6. Transfer the sandwich to the air fryer oven and bake for 5 to 7 minutes.
7. Serve immediately.

Nutrition:Calories 311 Fat 11g Carbohydrate 22g Protein 31g

56. Lettuce Fajita Meatball Wraps

Preapration Time:10 minutes

Cooking Time: 10 minutes

Servings: 4

Ingredients:

- 1 pound (454 g) 85% lean ground beef
- ½ cup salsa, plus more for serving
- ¼ cup chopped onions
- ¼ cup diced green or red bell peppers
- 1 large egg, beaten
- 1 teaspoon fine sea salt
- ½ teaspoon chili powder
- ½ teaspoon ground cumin
- 1 clove garlic, minced
- Cooking spray
- For Serving:
- 8leaves Boston lettuce
- Pico de gallo or salsa
- Lime slices

Directions:

1. Spray the air fryer basket with cooking spray.
2. In a large bowl, mix together all the Ingredients:until well combined.
3. Shape the meat mixture into eight 1-inch balls. Place the meatballs in the air fryer basket, leaving a little space between them.
4. Select the Air Fry function and cook at 350 degrees Fahrenheit (177 degrees Celsius) for 10 minutes, or until cooked through

and no longer pink inside and the internal temperature reaches 145 degrees Fahrenheit (63 degrees Celsius).

5. Serve each meatball on a lettuce leaf, topped with pico de gallo or salsa. Serve with lime slices.

Nutrition:Calories 576 Fat 49g Total Carbohydrates 8g Fiber 2g Protein 25g

57. Easy Homemade Hamburgers

Preapration Time:5 minutes

Cooking Time: 15 minutes

Servings: 2

Ingredients:

- 3/4 pound lean ground chuck
- Kosher salt and ground black pepper, to taste
- 3tablespoons onion, minced
- 1 teaspoon garlic, minced
- 1 teaspoon soy sauce
- 1/2 teaspoon smoked paprika
- 1/4 teaspoon ground cumin
- 1/2 teaspoon cayenne pepper
- 1/2 teaspoon mustard seeds
- 2burger buns

Directions:

1. Thoroughly combine the ground chuck, salt, black pepper, onion, garlic and soy sauce in a mixing dish.
2. Season with smoked paprika, ground cumin, cayenne pepper and mustard seeds. Mix to combine well.
3. Shape the mixture into 2 equal patties.
4. Spritz your patties with a nonstick cooking spray. Air fry your burgers at 380 degrees F for about 11 minutes or to your desired degree of doneness.
5. Place your burgers on burger buns and serve with favorite toppings. Devour!

Nutrition: Calories 433 Fat 17.4g Carbohydrates 40g Protein 39.2g Sugars 6.4g

58. Easy Beef Burritos

Preapration Time: 5 minutes

Cooking Time: 25 minutes

Servings: 3

Ingredients:

- 1 pound rump steak
- Sea salt and crushed red pepper, to taste
- 1/2 teaspoon shallot powder
- 1/2 teaspoon porcini powder
- 1/2 teaspoon celery seeds
- 1/2 teaspoon dried Mexican oregano
- 1 teaspoon piri Piri powder
- 1 teaspoon lard, melted
- 3(approx 7-8" dia) whole-wheat tortillas

Directions:

1. Toss the rump steak with the spices and melted lard.
2. Cook in your Air Fryer at 390 degrees Fahrenheit for 20 minutes, turning it halfway through the cooking Time. Place on a cutting board to cool slightly.
3. Slice against the grain into thin strips.
4. Spoon the beef strips onto wheat tortillas; top with your favorite fixings, roll them up and serve. Enjoy!

Nutrition: Calories 368 Fat 13g Carbohydrates 20.2g Protein 35.1g Sugars 2.7g

59. Beef Parmigiana Sliders

Preapration Time:5 minutes

Cooking Time: 15 minutes

Servings: 2

Ingredients:

- 1/2 pound lean ground chuck
- 1 ounce bacon bits
- 2tablespoons tomato paste
- 3tablespoons shallots, chopped
- 1 garlic clove, minced
- 1/4 cup parmesan cheese, grated
- 1 teaspoon cayenne pepper
- Salt and black pepper, to taste
- 4pretzel rolls

Directions:

1. Thoroughly combine the ground chuck, bacon bits, tomato paste, shallots, garlic, parmesan cheese, cayenne pepper, salt, black pepper.
2. Shape the mixture into 4 equal patties.
3. Spritz your patties with a nonstick cooking spray. Air fry your burgers at 380 degrees Fahrenheit for about 11 minutes or to your desired degree of doneness.
4. Place your burgers on pretzel rolls and serve with favorite toppings. Enjoy!

Nutrition: Calories 516 Fat 20.7g Carbohydrates 42g Protein 34.3g Sugars 5.1g

60. Chicago-Style Beef Sandwich

Preapration Time:5 minutes

Cooking Time: 25 minutes

Servings: 2

Ingredients:

- 1/2 pound chuck, boneless
- 1 tablespoon olive oil
- 1 tablespoon soy sauce
- 1/4 teaspoon ground bay laurel
- 1/2 teaspoon shallot powder
- 1/4 teaspoon porcini powder
- 1/2 teaspoon garlic powder
- 1/2 teaspoon cayenne pepper
- Kosher salt and ground black pepper, to taste
- 1 cup pickled vegetables, chopped
- 2ciabatta rolls, sliced in half

Directions:

1. Toss the chuck roast with olive oil, soy sauce and spices until well coated.
2. Cook in the preheated Air Fryer at 400 degrees Fahrenheit for 20 minutes, turning over halfway through the cooking Time.
3. Shred the meat with two forks and adjust seasonings.
4. Top the bottom halves of the ciabatta rolls with a generous portion of the meat and pickled vegetables. Place the tops of the ciabatta rolls on the sandwiches. Serve immediately and enjoy!

Nutrition: Calories 385 Fat 17.4g Carbohydrates 28.1g Protein 29.8g Sugars 6.2g

CPSIA information can be obtained
at www.ICGtesting.com
Printed in the USA
BVHW090231260621
610448BV00003B/1042